WHAT EATS WHAT IN A RAIN FOREST FOOD CHAIN

ILLUSTRATED BY ANNE WERTHEIM

WRITTEN BY LISA J. AMSTUTZ

PICTURE WINDOW BOOKS
a capstone imprint

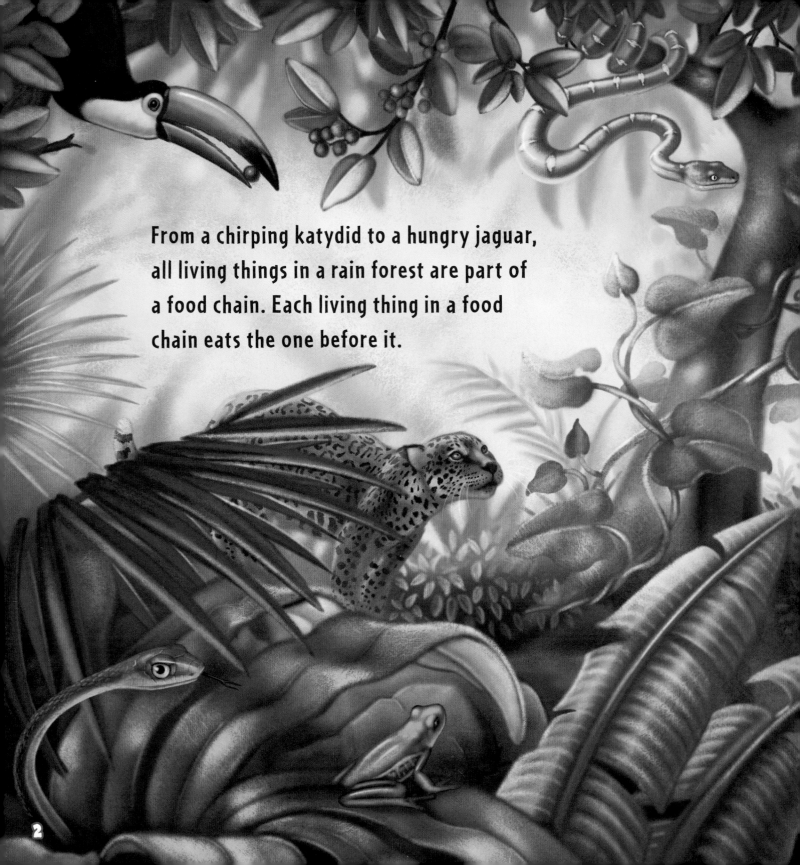

From a chirping katydid to a hungry jaguar, all living things in a rain forest are part of a food chain. Each living thing in a food chain eats the one before it.

producer

Almost all food chains rely on the sun. In the rain forest, the sun shines down on the silky leaves of a cacao tree.

Producers use sunlight, water, nutrients, and air to make their own food.

A katydid nibbles the cacao leaf. This insect is hard to spot. Its green wings look like a leaf.

consumer, herbivore

A consumer eats plants or animals for energy. An herbivore eats only plants.

A hungry tree frog sees the katydid move.
Zap! He shoots out his long, sticky tongue.
What a tasty snack for a tree frog!

consumer,
carnivore

8

A carnivore eats only other animals.

The tree frog blends in with the leaves.
But a blue-crowned motmot eyes it.

consumer,
omnivore

The bird snatches
the frog.

An omnivore eats both
plants and animals.

consumer,
carnivore

An emerald tree boa hangs from a branch. When the motmot flies by, the snake makes its move.

A jaguar is hungry.
It stalks the snake ...

The jaguar is a powerful hunter, but it doesn't live forever. One day the jaguar has a deadly fall. A king vulture finds the cat's body and feeds.

consumer, scavenger

A scavenger eats mainly dead plants or animals.

Insects, bacteria, and fungi feed on what's left of the jaguar's body.

decomposers

Decomposers break down dead plants and animals. Their waste is used as nutrients by plants.

Nutrients from the jaguar's body will return to the soil. In spring a new cacao tree will grow in this soil. And the food chain will continue.

FOOD WEB

You've seen a food chain in action. Now take a look at this food web of the Amazon rain forest. A food web is made up of many food chains that are found in one place.

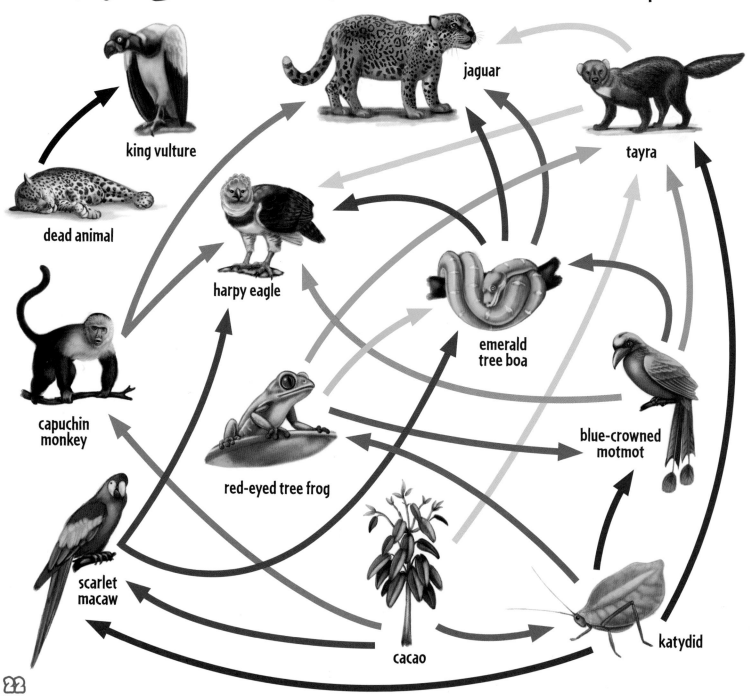

king vulture

dead animal

jaguar

tayra

harpy eagle

capuchin monkey

emerald tree boa

red-eyed tree frog

blue-crowned motmot

scarlet macaw

cacao

katydid

GLOSSARY

bacteria—tiny living things that exist all around you and inside you; some bacteria cause disease

carnivore—an animal that eats only other animals

consumer—an animal that eats plants or animals for energy

decomposer—a living thing, such as fungi or bacteria, that breaks down dead plants or animals

food web—many food chains connected to one another

fungus—a living thing similar to a plant but without leaves, flowers, or roots

herbivore—an animal that eats only plants

nutrient—a part of food, like a vitamin, that is used for growth

omnivore—an animal that eats both plants and animals

producer—a plant that uses sunlight, water, nutrients, and air to grow

rain forest—a thick forest where a great deal of rain falls

scavenger—an animal that feeds mainly on dead plants or animals

READ MORE

Amstutz, Lisa J. *Rain Forest Animal Adaptations.* Amazing Animal Adaptations. Mankato, Minn.: Capstone Press, 2012.

Benoit, Peter. *Tropical Rain Forests.* A True Book. New York: Children's Press, 2011.

Simon, Seymour. *Tropical Rainforests.* New York: HarperCollinsPublishers, 2010.

INTERNET SITES

FactHound offers a safe, fun way to find Internet sites related to this book. All of the sites on FactHound have been researched by our staff.

Here's all you do:

Visit *www.facthound.com*

Type in this code: 9781404873872

Super-cool stuff! Check out projects, games and lots more at **www.capstonekids.com**

INDEX

LOOK FOR ALL THE BOOKS IN THE FOOD CHAINS SERIES:

WHAT EATS WHAT IN A
DESERT FOOD CHAIN

WHAT EATS WHAT IN A
FOREST FOOD CHAIN

WHAT EATS WHAT IN A
RAIN FOREST FOOD CHAIN

WHAT EATS WHAT IN AN
OCEAN FOOD CHAIN

Thanks to our advisers for their expertise, research, and advice:
Kelly Swing, PhD
Founding Director of the Tiputini Biodiversity Station
Universidad San Francisco de Quito

Terry Flaherty, PhD, Professor of English
Minnesota State University, Mankato

Editor: Shelly Lyons
Designer: Alison Thiele
Art Director: Nathan Gassman
Production Specialist: Danielle Ceminsky
The illustrations in this book were created digitally.

Picture Window Books
1710 Roe Crest Drive
North Mankato, MN 56003
www.capstonepub.com

Library of Congress Cataloging-in-Publication Data
Amstutz, Lisa J.
  What eats what in a rain forest food chain / by Lisa J. Amstutz ; Illustrations by Anne Wertheim.
     p. cm.—(Capstone Picture Window Books: food chains)
  Includes index.
ISBN 978-1-4048-7387-2 (library binding)
ISBN 978-1-4048-7694-1 (paperback)
ISBN 978-1-4048-7983-6 (ebook PDF)
1. Rain forest ecology—Juvenile literature. 2. Rain forest animals—Juvenile literature. 3. Food chains (Ecology)—Juvenile literature. I. Wertheim, Anne, ill. II. Title.

QH541.5.R27A53 2013
577.34—dc23

2012001233

Printed in the United States of America in North Mankato, Minnesota.
042012   006682CGF12